Annunciations

Poems out of Scripture

Annunciations

Poems out of Scripture

by

Kathleen Henderson Staudt

Mellen Poetry Press
Lewiston Queenston Lampeter

Library of Congress Cataloging-in-Publication Data

Staudt, Kathleen Henderson, 1953-
    Annunciations : poems out of scripture / Kathleen Henderson Staudt.
        p. cm.
    ISBN 0-7734-3488-7
        1. Bible--History of Biblical events--Poetry. 2. Religious poetry, American. I. Title.

PS3619.T4754A84 2003
811'.54--dc21

2003041227

Copyright © 2003 Kathleen Henderson Staudt

All rights reserved. For information contact

<table>
<tr><td>The Edwin Mellen Press
Box 450
Lewiston, New York
USA 14092-0450</td><td>The Edwin Mellen Press
Box 67
Queenston, Ontario
CANADA L0S 1L0</td></tr>
</table>

The Edwin Mellen Press, Ltd.
Lampeter, Ceredigion, Wales
UNITED KINGDOM SA48 8LT

Printed in the United States of America

Table of Contents

Preface and Acknowledgements……………………….............iii

I. In the Cool of the Evening
In the Cool of the Evening…………………………….............5

II. Annunciations
Annunciations…………………………………………….............12

Judgment Day………………………………………………….16

Sarah Laughed……………………………………………….19

A Gloss on Sarah's Laughter………………………………….20

On the Way to Bethlehem……..……………………………….23

Holy Innocents…………………………………………..25

Holy Night……………………………………………………….27

Servants at Cana………………………………………............30

Jairus…………………………………………………………….33

On the Way to the House of Jairus……………………………….35

The Daughter of Jairus………………………….....…………….38

Peter, Back in the Boat…………………………………......…41

Martha………………………………………………………….43

Gesthemane..46

Thomas...49

The Beloved Disciple at the Cross 52

An Idle Tale..56

Another Annunciation..60

EmmausTraveler..63

Mary Magdalene at the Tomb...65

The Embrace in the Garden..67

Going and Telling..69

Holy Spirit...71

The Spirit and the Bride...73

III Evensong: 2001
Washington National Cathedral,
October 7, 2001...76

Evensong...80

Preface and Acknowledgements

> *Aren't there annunciations*
> *Of one sort or another*
> *In most lives?*
>   *Denise Levertov*

    In the Biblical story of the Annunciation, Mary says "yes" to the angel's baffling invitation to her to bear God into the world in the form of a human child. The poet Denise Levertov, in her poetic midrash on this story, suggests that Mary's "yes" to the angel can be an invitation to all of us. I have called these poems "annunciations" because in various ways they respond to an invitation to meet and receive the holy in the midst of ordinary life. Drawing on stories from Scripture, they reflect ways of saying "yes" (and sometimes "no") to the mystery that reveals itself in the depths of human experiences and relationships: in the giving and enjoyment of bodily life, in brokenness and grieving, in healing and in hope.

    In the rabbinic tradition of midrash, the interpretation of Scripture uncovers new voices and meanings in the familiar words of a sacred text, and so it contributes to an ongoing and ever-expanding tradition of conversation between humanity and God. Many of these poems engage in the imaginative process of midrash. Some also draw on Christian contemplative practices of meditation where one imaginatively "enters" a passage from Scripture, becoming a character, experiencing the setting, and entering into conversations in order to discover new dimensions of the story, and thus to become more aware of where the divine life meets and enters our everyday life and work.

    To orient the reader, I have provided the relevant Biblical passages on the page preceding each poem. Unless otherwise noted, these Biblical quotations are from the Revised Standard Version of the Bible (1946, 1952, Division of Christian Education of the National Council of Churches of Christ in the USA). This is the version I have read and heard since childhood, and so whose music is most familiar to me. Occasionally I have used the more inclusive language of the New Revised Standard Version (NRSV: 1993, Harper Collins Publishers). My epigraph is from Denise Levertov's poem "Annunciation," in *A Door in the Hive* (New Directions, 1989). My poem entitled "Another Annunciation" takes its inspiration from the Spiritual Exercises of St. Ignatius of Loyola, #218-224, as rendered by David Fleming, S.J. in *Draw Me Into Your Friendship: The Spiritual Exercises* (St. Louis: Institute of Jesuit Sources, 1996).

    I would like to thank the *Anglican Theological Review* for permission to reprint "Sarah Laughed"(Summer 1993), "The Embrace in the Garden," and portions of "On the Way to the House of Jairus" and "The Beloved Disciple at the Cross" (Summer 2002) I also thank *The Living Church* for permission to reprint "Evensong" (April 2002). I am particularly grateful to Margaret Adams Parker for her permission to use a detail from her woodcut, "The Sacrifice of Isaac" in the cover design, and to Alexandra Dorr for the photograph. Special thanks to my husband Lou, for his meticulous care in helping complete the the cover design, and for our life together.

Kathleen Henderson Staudt

Annunciations

Poems out of Scripture

I: In the Cool of the Evening

And they heard the sound of the Lord God walking in the garden in the cool of the day, and the man and his wife hid themselves from the presence of the Lord God among the trees of the garden.
Genesis 3:8-9

*

In the Cool of the Evening

Every evening I come here, and draw you to my breast
    What you have noticed today?
I am waiting to hear, for everything you find
    Is fresh and new to you, never seen this way before.
As you tell me about it, Creation grows richer.
And we celebrate together
    In heart's joy and dancing,
        Here in this garden
        In the cool of the evening.

Have you noticed
    How the tiny white violets open to the sun
    and close at evening?
Have you tasted the freshness of ripened grapes, or berries,
fresh from the vine
    Or smelled   Tell me what you have smelled!
Have you been to the sea's shore yet, and have you noticed
    How smoothly the sandpipers skim before the waves
Or how the pelican hovers, then lets go and plunges--sinking her
heart into the sea, where she is fed?
Have you heard the sea swell pound and seen the
        Waves crest, pink in the sunrise?

Have you noticed yet
A pulsing beat, all through you
This is life:
    My gift to you.

And as each day there is evening and there is morning
So you will know

      the ebb and flow
of this great pulse.

When it is filling you, you will be strong and eager
    And run out to me boldly
    And leap for joy.

And sometimes this force of life will wane in you
    and you will know
It is time to rest with me awhile.
And I will be glad to welcome you here.

So there will be
    mornings and evenings,
      turnings and passages, and I in all of them.

I am waiting to hear of the first time you notice
The trembling joy of bodies meeting,
        flesh touching flesh.
And how in that union, everything joins and dances, and dances,
and dances.

It is not good
    That you should be alone.
I will make more of you
    more of you, yet out of you
Each new person will be part of one before,
    Yet also new,
        glorious, separate.
So each of you will be
      one flesh with all the others
And all will be one body with the earth that brought you forth.

And as in one another
You see yourselves, and not yourselves
So each new meeting, each new friendship,
Will carry in it more of me
As in each new person, each new way of love
   I come again among you.

When you feel a new life growing within you
   Sharing your flesh, swimming and frolicking
   held within you, and a part of you.
You will know, from the nearness of this growing life
How I am bound to you, and each of you to me.

Wait until you see
   the tiny toes and fingers
The fresh-born miracle of a new child
   As now you come to me
each evening, for food and loving
So the children will come to you, and you will know
   the wonder of a fresh life
   Separate, yet of you
   Seeing more than you had noticed before.

There will be more of you, and they will find each other
And out of one another, bring forth more new lives,
and each one will be different,
   and you will love the differences!

Perhaps, when there are more of you
   You will learn to make
From all this variety of noises and voices
   Songs
And I shall be among you in the singing.

With more of you, there will be
Bodies at play, in games and dancing
You will stretch out arms and move your feet,
Turning and leaping, in patterns and figures
Pulsing to music, drumming a dance
Your bodies moving as my heart moves
Stretching and bounding, rejoicing with you.

I have made you to know it all
    Every detail of this Creation
    All that I have called "Good."

When will you learn the intricacies:
    Puzzles, numbers, patterns, shapes
The delight of randomness
The satisfaction
    Of order and equation?
I will teach you how, and as we gaze together
This living Creation, shifting and changing
infinite in its surprises,
            will unfold.
Your bodies
    cells and systems,
The universe itself, from tiniest particles
    to unimagined vastness.
I want you to know it all
For all of it is good.

I am waiting
for the first time you bring me
    something you have made, and say
"Look! I made this! It is for you."
And I will know your pleasure
And that you have known
    the joy of making, my deepest joy.

And so in fresh creation more will be added,
    And we will be joined:
In weaving and in making
    We will be joined.

Every evening, in the coolness, I come and walk
    and wait to see
What you have discovered
    As more and more, you wake up to the world.

I look for you now, running to me
    all aglow with news.
Come, leap to my embrace,
    Drink in my love.
        And tell me all of it.
Laughter shall spring out, and we shall watch creation grow
    And dance and feast together
    In the cool of the evening.

Come to me! Where are you?
    Why would you hide from me?

 O my beloved ones
    What is this
        What is this
        That you
            have done?

II. Annunciations

*

In the sixth month the angel Gabriel was sent from God to a town in Galilee named Nazareth, to a virgin engaged to a man whose name was Joseph, of the house of David; and the virgin's name was Mary. And he came to her and said, "Hail, O favored one! The Lord is with you." But she was greatly troubled by the saying, and considered in her mind what sort of greeting this might be.
Luke 1:26-29

Annunciations

The angel Gabriel, the story goes
Greeted our sister Mary
Exclaimed in loving wonder
How she was blessed, full of grace
Heralding the mystery
Of Word becoming flesh.

This same angel, another story goes
Embraced Muhammad, blessing him
(peace on him, believers say)
Giving him words he never could have known.

And perhaps it was the same
Who grasped the hand of Abraham,
Saying, Stop
        Do not sacrifice this child.

Speaking for the same God
Who said to Abraham,
        Go out to a new land
        And you shall be
        A blessing

Who spoke to Moses, saying
        I will set you free

Whose words Jesus was speaking when he said,
        You are
        a city on a hill
        Let your light
        Shine.

And who will tell the angel's grief
At so many embraces,
So many promises
Perverted by power

    Twisted

        Twisted

            Twisted?

∗

Then he will say to those at his left hand, "Depart from me, you cursed, into the eternal fire prepared for the devil and his angels; for I was hungry and you gave me no food, I was thirsty and you gave me no drink, I was a stranger and you did not welcome me, naked and you did not clothe me, sick and in prison and you did not visit me." Then they also will answer, "Lord, when did we see thee hungry or thirsty or a stranger or naked or sick or in prison, and did not minister to thee? Then he will answer them, "Truly, I say to you, as you did it not to one of the least of these, you did it not to me."

Matthew 25: 41-45

For God so loved the world that he gave his only Son, so that everyone who believes in him may not perish but may have eternal life.

John 3:16 (NRSV)

Judgment Day

The nightmare returns: It is 1981,
Inauguration Day, and on the television screens
The Good Guys are in. "Today the world is bright," they say.
Now we will be led by
People like us."
In the glare of celebration, whole neighborhoods dissolve
Off the screen, invisible,
Disappeared.

Walking toward the subway, from where I have been teaching
Young adults who never learned to read in school,
With sudden clarity, I see
Boarded-up houses,
Dazed and aimless men standing on corners.
A grandmother holds a child by one hand,
Dragging a half-full grocery cart.
A broken church marquee proclaims: JOHN 3:16:
AND GOD SO LOVE. .. . .

Though I ride this subway line, under decaying streets,
And come home to this block of shabby walk-ups,
I could blend in with those bright rulers and their wives.
Our apartment here is newly renovated.
My face is white, my clothes are new.
I am a "young professional"
Desirable tenants, we are just passing through.

The housekeeper has been here.
The walls seem whiter than I remembered,
Clean without my labor.
But on the gleaming window frame
A brown cockroach, the size of my thumb
Looks at me.

In this city, such creatures inhabit all our houses.
The rich use chemicals to remove them when they come.
The poor live with them, having no choice.
Reaching for the spray can, I forget for a moment
The colonies of his fellows
Who live within these walls, and under these streets,
And in my neighbors' houses.

Looking back at him,
I decide
Because I can decide
To let him live.

The son whom Sarah bore to him, Abraham named Isaac [That is, "He laughed"]. . . Sarah said, "God has given me good reason to laugh, and everyone who hears will laugh with me."
                                Genesis 21: 3, 6.   (NRSV)

*

Sarah Laughed

Listening at the tent flap
  While her husband talked to God
    She overheard the good news: At last
      (At ninety-whatever) She would have a child!

And she laughed.
  although, you might well say, it wasn't funny..
    The timing must have seemed a cruel joke.
What? Now that I am old, shall I have joy?
    Why now? Why not fifty, seventy years ago
      When she was strong and ready, even longing.
        Why wait to grant a lifetime's fervent prayer
          Until all hope was gone?

So listening at the flap, in joy and bitterness, she laughed,
Never dreaming that her husband's God
Might want to speak to her.

Her laughter, though, was heard,
And soon she trembled
To hear the strange, familiar, terrifying voice of God.
    And yet, that voice was also sharing in the joke
    In confidence, across the kitchen table.
"You laugh?" said God, and laughed when she denied it,
"I heard you laugh. But wait.
Wait, and I will show you.
Is anything too wonderful for Me?"
    "Just wait, and I will show you
And remember, how you laughed."

And Sarah's laughter, creature to Creator,
        named her child.

A Gloss on Sarah's Laughter

The timing always seems absurd. So it happened
In the midst of a young life
Loaded with the weary joys of others' growing times
I brushed against the angel of death
Just close enough to learn
How little I know of time.
As life was snatched away, then dangled and restored
A deeper longing opened
Calling out new words

And as the words began to come, I laughed
How could this be?
The timing seemed absurd.
When to find new words, with so much else to do:
Constant interruptions,
Phones to be answered, shopping to be done,
Swings to be pushed and buses to be met,
Stories to read and tell, cakes to be baked
Schedules to make, and break, and make again.

"You laugh?" said God, "just wait, and pay attention
    And I will teach you wonder."

Now there are new gifts, with strange instructions:
A distant celebration,
To be joined with all my heart.
A quiet "thank you" called out at the kitchen window
To be said while rinsing dishes, watching children play.
A half-remembered hymn, of wideness and mercy
To be sung aloud, while chopping vegetables.

Clothes to be collected, washed and dried
And folded in the quiet after bedtime
When solitude is welcome, luminous.
And stillness speaks, charged with a gracious presence.

So, between the cracks and chinks of noisy, messy life,
Grace rushes in, and time is found.
No wonder Sarah laughed, at that last-expected moment.
She laughed, and as I write these words
I laugh, too.

In those days a decree went out from Caesar Augustus that all the world should be enrolled. This was the first enrollment, when Quirinius was governor of Syria. And all went to be enrolled, each to his own city. And Joseph also went up from Galilee, from the city of Nazareth, to the city of David, which is called Bethlehem, because he was of the house and lineage of David, to be enrolled with Mary, his betrothed, who was with child. And while they were there, the time came for her to be delivered.

Luke 2: 1-6

*

On the Way to Bethlehem

The timing could not be worse
But it's the law. My husband has to go,
Even though I'm well along.
You are lively within me, moving and kicking me.
It hurts, Waking me in the night,
Reminding me, as I walk
More and more laboriously,
You are coming soon.

I suppose we are safe enough
After all, it was an angel who came.
Looking back, I have never doubted that.
My husband has been tender, despite my disgrace.
He is sure, too, about the angel.
So I suppose we have no cause to worry.
It's only my aching back
The sharp pains from your tiny feet,
The smell and press of crowds, and all the delays.

The only thing that matters now, is bearing you safely
Into this messy world
And even that I cannot control now.
I did what I could do, but it's all left behind.
At home, we had a place prepared for you.
I longed to see you soon.
Then I hoped you would come later, after our return
But now I know for sure that you will be coming
To a place we did not know.

I catch my breath at a sudden squeeze of pain.
My body recognizes the agony,
Already begun.

*

Then Herod, when he saw that he had been tricked by the wise men, was in a furious rage, and he sent and killed all the male children in Bethlehem and in all that region who were two years old or under, according to the time which he had ascertained from the wise men. Then was fulfilled what was spoken by the prophet Jeremiah:

> A voice was heard in Ramah,
> wailing and loud lamentation
> Rachel weeping for her children
> she refused to be consoled
> because they were no more."

Matthew 2:16-18
Jeremiah 31:15

*

Holy Innocents

      We will kill their children
        As they have killed our children
Says the voice on the radio
From the Middle East
I forget which side. Meanwhile
Eyes gaze out
From newspaper pages, or television screens
The eyes of dying children,
Of mothers who know what is happening
Men gone, homes destroyed, bodies brutalized
Their molten grief and anger, defiant, shields
      Desecrated life
.
They seek a human face that will meet this gaze
A gaze that will see the faces behind
The words we read on the page, hear on the news:
      Collateral
      Unintended
They are facing down the Crusaders' god,
The god of Us and Them, who says
I am on your side, against those others.
I will crush your enemies
Murder their children
Support you at all costs
Love you. Hate Them.

Where did we lose
the God no one owns
Who broods over our thriving
Like the mother shielding her threatened child
Whose fierce judgment speaks
Out of these wise eyes?

*

But Mary kept all these things, pondering them in her heart. . . .
                              Luke 2:19

*

Holy Night

Wisdom, sparkling in your infant eyes, at play
From before all ages, gazes up at me now
Across my breast. Your baby smile
Delights to meet mine, your tiny hands
Touch my skin, grasp my finger.
Our gazes hold each other in ancient love
Wisdom, sparkling in your infant eyes, at play.

Whose joy is it, mine or yours
When your strong, tiny lips at last draw out
Milk I have been bursting to give you.
Aching with abundance, my swollen breasts
Let down gladly the food that only you can take,
When you receive what my body longed to give you
Whose joy is it, mine or yours?

You and I are the only ones awake
Fed and rested, and now you want to play.
Standing in my lap, pulling on my hands, crowing
Delighted in your growing strength.
Your eyes meet mine, and we hold one another
Suspended in time, in the friendly quiet
Where you and I are the only ones awake.

*

On the third day there was a marriage at Cana in Galilee, and the mother of Jesus was there; Jesus also was invited to the marriage, with the disciples. When the wine failed, the mother of Jesus said to him, "They have no wine." And Jesus said to her, "O woman, what have you to do with me? My hour has not yet come." His mother said to the servants, "Do whatever he tells you." Now six stone jars were standing there, for the Jewish rites of purification, each holding twenty or thirty gallons. Jesus said to them, "Fill the jars with water." And they filled them up to the brim. He said to them, "Now draw some out, and take it to the steward of the feast." So they took it. When the steward of the feast tasted the water now become wine, and did not know where it came from (though the servants who had drawn the water knew), the steward of the feast called the bridegroom and said, "Every man serves the good wine first; but you have kept the good wine until now." This, the first of his signs, Jesus did at Cana in Galilee, and manifested his glory; and his disciples believed in him."

John 2: 1-11

*

Servants at Cana

The servants know what happened.
We were the ones who saw the wine run out
We knew it would.
We were the ones with aching backs
Called on to draw water
When the problem was
We were out of wine.

You could feel the strain in the air
As guests found out
We were out of wine
Some of the important ones left.
We knew they would.
The host afraid of being thought stingy
The party threatening to break up.

No wonder the woman was so urgent
As she told her son
They have no wine.
Ordering us to do
Whatever he told us to.
No matter, as we hauled the water,
Following this silly command,
He, with his hands on the jars,
Began to smile at us
As if he were bringing a surprise
Just for us
As if we were not servants, but invited guests
At a party of our own.

And now, the wine steward discovers
The best wine, where only now

We were pouring water.
We knew what had happened, tasted and saw
The bridegroom poured it out, the festivities began
With the few guests who had stayed and now
More of us servants than guests
The wonder-working man seemed to be our host
Inviting us both to drink and to dance
Servants and guests, all mingling together.

There is something new about this wine
So strong and sweet, the best ever
For drawing a party together
It calls us, guests and servants,
Bridegroom and bride
To dancing.

Radiant singing invites our voices
And dancing is everywhere, weaving among us
A hand squeezes mine, and my body follows
And music is throbbing
Lilting with joy
Propelling us faster.

Abandoned to following, drawn into dancing
Weaving through figures with new-known friends
Hands reaching out pull in other dancers
Given to whirling
Given to dancing
Swirled to a center where all of us fit
Enfolded in laughter
Music surrounding
Joined at the wedding feast
Home
In the dance.

*

And there came a man named Jairus, who was a ruler of the synagogue; and falling at Jesus' feet, he besought him to come to his house, for he had an only daughter, about twelve years of age, and she was dying.

Luke 8:41-2

*

Jairus

No. This will not happen
In my family. Other people's children
Sicken, die. But not my daughter.
My delight, my joy.

Fortunately, in my position
I have connections. I can find her
The best healer around.
He may be controversial, but he can't be stupid.
He will know who I am, and God knows he could use
Some friends in higher places.

Make way. Coming through.
We are in a hurry.
Make way for the healer
And the important man
Push through these crowds. Don't you know
Who I am, and what a help I could be to you?

All these people are slowing us down
So many hands, so many stinking bodies
Pressing up against us.
Fingers groping out of piles of ragged clothing
Arms and legs, covered with dirt, oozing sores
Blood.
And they all want to touch him

A few crazies
Run off, shouting, believing they've been healed.
Please, get past these people. It may be
Too late already.
Make way.   Hurry.
Please.

*

As he went, the people pressed around him. And a woman who had had a flow of blood for twelve years and could not be healed by any one, came up behind him, and touched the fringe of his garment; and immediately her flow of blood ceased. And Jesus said, "Who was it that touched me?" When all denied it, Peter said, "Master the multitudes surround you and press upon you! But Jesus said, "Some one touched me; for I perceive that power has gone forth from me." And when the woman saw that she was not hidden, she came trembling, and falling down before him declared in the presence of all the people why she had touched him, and how she had been immediately healed. And he said to her, "Daughter, your faith has made you well; go in peace."

Luke 8: 42-4

*

On the Way to the House of Jairus

If I could just touch
    the hem of his garment,
        I could keep hidden,
    and still be healed
He doesn't need to know
I am here.

I'm good at this hiding
After twelve years bleeding,
    Twelve years swindled from me
    Twelve years concealing
    the disgrace of what I am
I must keep hidden
Everyone knows
Women may not bleed in the presence of men.

Why has he stopped? How can he ask,
    "Who touched me?"
It could be anyone
    I could still keep
    hidden

But
something new is drawing me
    And I know
I will step out now,
    In front of everyone
And speak.

*

While he was still speaking, a man from the ruler's house came and said, "Your daughter is dead; do not trouble the teacher any more." But Jesus on hearing this answered him, "Do not fear; only believe, and she shall be well." And when he came to the house, he permitted no one to enter with him, except Peter and John and James, and the father and mother of the child. And all were weeping and bewailing her; but he said, "Do not weep; for she is not dead but sleeping." And they laughed at him, knowing that she was dead. But taking her by the hand he called, saying "Child, arise." And her spirit returned, and she got up at once, and he directed that something should be given her to eat. And her parents were amazed; but he charged them to tell no one what had happened.

Luke 8: 49-5

*

The Daughter of Jairus

I hear my mother weeping.
She is clinging to my hand.
   A doorway is opening,
    and my other hand reaches
      Out into light.
        Grasping another hand reaching to me.
A voice calls out in love:
"Little girl, arise."

I know that voice out of the light.
I have heard it
   In the quiet of the evening garden, under the olive trees
   When the warm breeze has brushed through my hair
   And the bird-songs hushed, as if someone were there.
I have heard it in my baby brother's shouts of wonder
   When he offered me a flower, or a shining stone.
I have heard it in the great assembly at the temple
   Where they sang of loving kindness, enduring forever.

I know that voice.
I begin to see his face.
A man's face, as I see it,
   The face of one invisible friend
   Known since infancy, never named or seen,
   Though we were everywhere together.
He holds my hand and leads me through the door
   Into a light like none I have ever seen
And yet familiar, filled with people
   Known, unknown and new-known.
Dancing and singing,
They welcome me with joy.

His hand is grasping mine now, and I look into the light
    "Child, arise", he says
And my eyes are opened, and I recognize his face.
I hear my parents weeping.
And I rise.

*

And in the fourth watch of the night he came to them, walking on the sea. But when the disciples saw him walking on the sea, they were terrified, saying, "It is a ghost!" And they cried out for fear. But immediately he spoke to them, saying, "Take heart, it is I; have no fear."

And Peter answered him, "Lord, if it is you, bid me come to you on the water." He said, "Come." So Peter got out of the boat and walked on the water and came to Jesus; but when he saw the wind, he was afraid and beginning to sink he cried out, "Lord, save me." Jesus immediately reached out his hand and caught him, saying to him, "O man of little faith, why did you doubt?" And when they got into the boat, the wind ceased."
Matthew 14: 25-32

*

Peter, Back in the Boat

It was the joy that drew me: the joy in your eyes,
When I said, "if it is you, bid me come across the water."
That must have been what made me think I could step out
Walking over waves I had not expected.
      I forgot
The pounding of the storm, the walls of water
Drawn by your eyes, your outstretched arm.

Only when I looked away, the waves came over me.
Now, fished out, dried off, back in the boat
Here, with our friends, and work to do,
I remember
The joy in your eyes.

*

When Jesus arrived, he found that Lazarus had already been in the tomb four days. Now Bethany was near Jerusalem, some two miles away, and many of the Jews had come to Martha and Mary to console them about their brother. When Martha heard that Jesus was coming, she went and met him, while Mary stayed at home. Martha said to Jesus, "Lord, if you had been here, my brother would not have died. But even now I know that God will give you whatever you ask of him." Jesus said to her, "Your brother will rise again." Martha said to him, 'I know that he will rise again in the resurrection on the last day." Jesus said to her, "I am the resurrection and the life. Those who believe in me, even though they die, will live, and everyone who lives and believes in me will never die. Do you believe this? She said to him, "Yes, Lord, I believe that you are the Messiah, the Son of God, the one coming into the world.

John 11: 21-27 (NRSV)

Jesus said, "Take away the stone." Martha, the sister of the dead man, said to him, "Lord, already there is a stench because he has been dead four days.

John 11: 39 (NRSV)

*

Martha

I have prayed, for days, that you would return to us
And you did not come.
If you had been here, my brother would not have died.
Where were you?
Surely you knew.
Why didn't you come to see us when there was time?

Now you are here.
Too late.   And yet,
With you standing right here, my answer is sure
Anger, pain and all.
With you here,
Bigger than life, stronger than death,
I can respond
   In spite of the stench,
   In spite of it being
   four days later,
   In spite of you not being here
   When we needed you.

In spite of all this, when you stand there and say, "I am
Resurrection. I am life. Do you believe this?"
With you standing right there,
I have
   No other answer.

*

He came out and went, as was his custom, to the Mount of Olives; and the disciples followed him. And when he reached the place, he said to them, "Pray that you may not come into the time of trial." Then he withdrew from them about a stone's throw, knelt down, and prayed, "Father, if you are willing, remove this cup from me; yet, not my will but yours be done." Then an angel from heaven appeared to him and gave him strength. In his anguish he prayed more earnestly, and his sweat became like great drops of blood falling down on the ground.

Luke 22: 39-44 (NRSV)

*

Gesthemane

Nothing more human than the fear
Racing heartbeat, crushing breath
Sweat breaking out cold under eyes
and armpits
Drenching the back
So overwhelming, you can hardly find voice
To say, help   Please
Anything but this

Nothing works.
None of the usual ways back to peace
So carefully prepared in calmer times:
Not the familiar place of regular retreat
Not these companions,
Paralyzed themselves,
Running away, or stupefied
You can hear it
Echo in them: No No No No
Not this.
Not now. No.

Just take it away, you beg,
Pushing back the cup of sorrow,
Saying, *Abba*, Maker of Me, please, no
Unless this is absolutely what you want,
And how could you?

Uttering this prayer, do you, perhaps, remember
As a distant vision, three companions
Rejoicing together at a glowing table,
So connected, so gathered into love,
They are as one?

And One who has your voice saying,
heart to heart, as on a shared breath,
I will drink this cup, knowing that if I do
The drinking of it will bring back to our heart
Companions we have lost,
And long to find again.

But do you know what this means?
Says One to You, tenderly,
Yourself to Yourself,
You will enter separation, you will know
The fear that grips the flesh.
And you will be left
To heartbreaking brutality
Desertion by companions,
Loneliness so deep, you will barely be able
To believe
Or utter
The *Abba* that joins us.

You may try to pray
And all that will remain will be
A distant, barely graspable, memory of love
Dripping sweat, gasping pulse
Pleading for deliverance.
Longing for companions.
Aching isolation, darkness
Friends asleep, betrayal near,
Alone, bathed in sweat and
Fear.

*

Thomas, called the Twin, said to his fellow disciples, "Let us also go, that we may die with him."
John 11:16

But Thomas (who was called the Twin), one of the twelve, was not with them when Jesus came. So the other disciples told him, "We have seen the Lord." But he said to them, "Unless I see in his hands the print of the nails, and place my finger in the mark of the nails, and place my hand in his side, I will not believe."
John 20: 24-5

*

Thomas

I was ready to die with you
Sharing your passion for justice,
Relying on your radiating strength.
I saw that your ideas
Could save us, believed
You would somehow overcome

And then, you let yourself be caught
By plain brutality, bureaucrats, stupidity.
Why couldn't you preserve yourself more sensibly?
Couldn't you see we needed you here?
The waste of it, finally, was too much for me.

The waste of it, to see you subject yourself
To taunts of bigoted soldiers, indifference
Of slimy politicians.
I trusted your strength, and now I am hating,
Hating those who caught you,
Furious with you.

Nothing will make this right.
I don't care if the whole world says
They have witnessed a miracle, and you are alive.
I could not believe this
Unless you came back, yourself, to give me what I need.

I already trusted too much. It broke my heart.
I will not believe it again.

*

So the soldiers did this. But standing by the cross of Jesus were his mother, and his mother's sister, Mary the wife of Clopas, and Mary Magdalene. When Jesus saw his mother and the disciple whom he loved standing beside her, he said to his mother, "Woman, behold your son." Then he said to the disciple, "Behold your mother." And from that hour the disciple took her to his own home.

John 19: 25-9

*

The Beloved Disciple at the Cross

You were so sure about this.
Praying for us, promising
You would not leave us
Desolate.
Hard to believe that now.

I could not bear to think of you
Laying down your life
Even though
Your eyes implored me, heart to heart, in friendship
Desperate
For someone to understand
How this could be an act of love.
I am trying.   It is
Hard.

My own great love
Must let you go, must even, in friendship
Rejoice with you
That your hour has come.
But down here, watching you die
I see only ugliness,
Hard wood, hard nails
Hardened hearts.

A routine inhumanity
Dominates this day.
As if, when they condemned you,
All compassion fled.
Leaving us, your friends, confused,
Appalled

Yes, you tried to help us understand.
You have told us
You are who You are:
Love-giver, Life creator,
Living here among us
Here, where one living person is able
> To drive a nail
> Into the hand
> of another.

How could we have imagined such a God,
Coming to the hammerers
With out-stretched hands?

*

But on the first day of the week, at early dawn, they came to the tomb, taking the spices that they had prepared. They found the stone rolled away from the tomb, but when they went in, they did not find the body. While they were perplexed about this, suddenly two men in dazzling clothes stood beside them. The women were terrified and bowed their faces to the ground, but the men said to them, "Why do you look for the living among the dead? He is not here, but has risen. Remember how he told you, while he was still in Galilee, that the Son of Man must be handed over to sinners, and be crucified, and on the third day rise again." Then they remembered his words, and returning from the tomb, they told all this to the eleven and to all the rest. Now it was Mary Magdalene, Joanna, Mary the mother of James and the other women with them who told this to the apostles. But these words seemed to them an idle tale, and they did not believe them.

Luke 24:1-11

*

An Idle Tale

We came with spices and tears
All of us wanting, one more time
To touch and lay to rest
Our Beloved Friend.
Missing him, weeping, yet wanting
That last farewell.
Dawn just beginning, and we smelled
The early scent of dust and dew,
Singing birds, their voices clear in pre-dawn silence
Especially the soothing coo of turtledoves
Echoing our quiet, inward tears.

It all changed so quickly.
We expected
Seal and stone, and found an open doorway.
Inside, where we should have found
Grey darkness and a new corpse,
All was light and voices.
The light beat onto me,
Caressing and warming, penetrating with its glow.
And in the light were His words
How He said He would rise again
And suddenly, we all understood:
Yes. It all made sense.

And our confusion told us
We were in the wrong place, for He was not there
And here we were, among the dead
And there is nothing in this tomb but light
And life.
All of us saw clearly, all at once.
Of course!

And our coming together was like the light
Illuminating, warming, lifting grief.
Even if I were blind, or struck wordless,
I would feel this light
Soak it in, like sunlight on wet skin.
Perhaps there are no words to say
How this is.
Perhaps they will have to see it for themselves
And this will seem to them
An idle tale.

*

When a woman is in travail she has sorrow, because her hour has come; but when she is delivered of the child, she no longer remembers the anguish, for joy that a child is born into the world. So you have sorrow now, but I will see you again and your hearts will rejoice, and no one will take your joy from you.

John 16: 21-2

*

Another Annunciation

Imagine, a story that didn't make it in,
But it must have been part of the story behind
The story we have.
Poets have to guess at these things.
While the other women bearing spices stood, bewildered
In the empty tomb
Knowing together what was really true
Wondering how they would explain
The light that had come to them,

Another scene must have been playing out.
Mary, his mother, living with his friend now
Sweeps the floor as dawn breaks.
Finally, blessedly alone, she lets the tears flow
As she remembers
The pitiful lightness of His dead body,
Down from the cross and stiffening in her arms,
Absurdly light, and helpless, the beloved light
No longer in his eyes
Gone.
Remembering again, his tiny body
Held to her breast, in a stinking, swept-clean stable
Remembering the day when it all started,
Herself a growing girl, sweeping the floor, as today
Staring at a pile of sweepings
As the room filled with light and the angel's voice said
"Hail, favored one!"

Now, again, she stares at the sweepings,
Glad of her tears, glad of the women who said
We'll go. You stay here. It has been enough for you.
And as her tears wet the dust, she knows

She is not alone
A voice says, gently, "Hail, favored one
Your Lord is with you" And she turns and sees
The twinkle in his eye that was always just for her.

He is laughing, delighted at her surprise
Yes. Really. I am here.
You knew I would come. I told you I would:
Remember?
She knows that body. Has held it in her arms.
Now she has to touch every inch of him
Count, as she did when he was new born
Every finger and toe
All there. There are wounds now. Dried blood
Deep holes
 Her fingers linger tenderly

But when she asks,"Does it hurt?" he simply laughs again
As a happy new mother would laugh, holding her child,
If you asked her, "Did it hurt?"
And you saw in her delight
The absurdity
Of that question.

He says to her:
If you asked a mother, gazing at her child
About the birthing moments before. If you asked her,
Did it hurt?
What would she say?
      Woman, what would she say?

*

That very day two of them were going to a village named Emmaus, about seven miles from Jerusalem, and talking with each other about all these things that had happened. While they were talking and discussing together, Jesus himself drew near and went with them. But their eyes were kept from recognizing him.

Luke 24: 13-16

*

Emmaus Traveler

The airport here in Frankfurt is bright at all hours.
This morning it is full of people, speaking, moving purposefully.
Tall, fair and focused, they pass me by.
I am newly arrived, unsure what time it is,
Knowing only where to go and wait,
and where to wash my face.

On the way, I meet a brown-skinned woman
Short, dressed in black and lace, dragging a lumpy bag.
She sees me seeing her, looks up, and grasps my arm.
"Sao Paolo?" she inquires. She expects me to know.
I meet her eyes and shake my head
 "No- no idea what plane."

Then I understand: the ocean she desires to cross,
I have just passed over.
"Sao Paolo – en Brasil?" I ask, in helpless Spanish.
"Si!" she rattles on, in excited Portuguese.
She sees I cannot understand.
But we have met each other.

Turning away, she meets my eye again,
	Raises fingers to her mouth
	 And blows a gentle kiss

*

But Mary stood weeping outside the tomb, and as she wept she stooped to look into the tomb; and she saw two angels in white, sitting where the body of Jesus had lain, one at the head and one at the feet. They said to her, "Woman, why are you weeping?" She said to them, "Because they have taken away my Lord, and I do not know where they have laid him."

John 20: 11-13

*

Mary Magdalene at the Tomb

The empty tomb
A vision of angels
But he is not here.
There is no one to ask:
Where have they laid him?
Where is he now?

The men who came with me have believed and gone away
Remembering his words.
The empty tomb
Enough for them.
They think they understand, have heard and seen
A vision of angels
But he is not here.
I came to touch, anoint with tears, one last time;
There is no one to ask:
Have you seen my Beloved?
Where have they laid him?
Where is he now?

What could console me?
Even if I saw,
in the empy tomb
A vision of angels,
They only show me what already I know:
He is not here.
There is no one to ask:
Have you seen my Beloved?
Who can tell me?
Where have they laid him?
Where is he now?

*

Saying this, she turned round and saw Jesus standing, but she did not know that it was Jesus. Jesus said to her, "Woman, why are you weeping? Whom do you seek?" Supposing him to be the gardener, she said to him, "Sir, if you have carried him away, tell me where you have laid him, and I will take him away." Jesus said to her, "Mary." She turned and said to him in Hebrew, "Rabboni!" (which means Teacher). Jesus said to her, "Do not hold me, for I have not yet ascended to the Father;

John 20:14-17

*

The Embrace in the Garden

How can you say, "Don't try to hold me?"

Wrenched from my weeping
Into your unreasonable joy
I heard you speak my name
Knew it was you
You, and more than you, more than I can grasp

But now, my cheek against your cheek,
Your hand stroking my hair,
I whisper the name I have always used for you
Rabboni!
        Mary!
Rabboni!

You whisper, delighted, of going and telling
But how could I not want to hold you here
Cheek against cheek,
Nail-scarred hands upon hair?

*

Jesus said to her, "Do not hold me, for I have not yet ascended to the Father; but go to my brethren and say to them, "I am ascending to my Father and your Father, to my God and your God."
Mary Magdalene went and said to the disciples, "I have seen the Lord"; and she told them that he had said these things to her.
John 20:17

*

Going and Telling

Go. Tell my friends. I am giving you the words. Tell them.
It is finished, and the new story has begun.
The body that holds you now
Alive and warm, is as real
As the body you saw mutilated,
Mocked, betrayed, brutalized.

Even though jeers drowned out the message
Of justice for the poor,
Release for the oppressed,
Unimagined forbearance,
Even though
It seems as though the promise I brought
Was pounded down
With the nails
They drove into these hands
Go and tell them:
They cannot kill it.

Step back. Take these wounded hands.
Clasp them in your own.
Gaze back at me, and see
The dancing in my eyes.
Now go.
Go and tell them
This life you are holding
Nothing can kill it.
Go. Go and tell them
You will see me
Again.

*

A new heart I will give you, and a new spirit I will put within you; and I will take out of your flesh the heart of stone and give you a heart of flesh.

Ezekiel 36: 26

*

Holy Spirit
For Marge

She came to meet me,
Beautiful and strong, and surging with desire:
"What do you want?" she asked me, a twinkle in her eye.
And timidly, I whispered: More.
A little more of this, please:
This springing-up of life, this beckoning mystery.
I want to enter more of it
Even the mud and mess.
More, I would like more, I whispered,
Then drew back.
But perhaps I want too much? I asked.
Am I too greedy?

HA! She shouted,
And her laughter boomed around me.
Look at you!
So drawn and self-controlled
You are
An anorexic at a banquet!
Come, and taste, and eat.
And when you've fattened up a bit,
I'll teach you how to dance!

And stretching out a spindly arm,
I reached for her rich fruits,
And began to taste, and eat.

*

I am my beloved's
> and his desire is for me.
Come, my beloved
> let us go forth into the fields
> and lodge in the villages;
let us go out early to the vineyards,
> and see whether the vines have budded,
whether the grape blossoms have opened
> and the pomegranates are in bloom
There I will give you my love.
The mandrakes give forth fragrance
> and over our doors are all choice fruits,
> new as well as old,
> which I have laid up for you, O my beloved.

> > > Song of Songs 7: 10-13

The Spirit and the Bride say, "Come."
> And let everyone who hears say,
> > "Come"
> And let everyone who is thirsty come,
> Let everyone who desires take the water of life as a gift.

> > > Revelation 22: 17

*

The Spirit and the Bride

This is no blushing bride, no veiled rosebud.
Bedecked, yes,
But not to hide her beauty.
Rather, gold and jewels, vivid colored silk
Reveal in freedom boldness of desire.
Lovers touch amid thickly perfumed blossoms
Sharing the sweetness of dripping fruit.

No hiding here. No retiring. No coyness:
The lover rejoices to unveil the bride.
She leaps to enjoy the embrace she fainted for
And the story ends in freedom.
Inviting, rejoicing:
The Spirit and the Bride say
Come!

III: Evensong 2001

*

In peace I will both lie down and sleep;
for thou alone, O Lord, makest me dwell in safety.
Psalm 4:8

*

Washington National Cathedral October 7, 2001

In Afghanistan today,
Our airplanes are dropping
Bombs and food
Too soon to know
Where this news will lead.

I walk the path where on Sundays in Eastertide,
Amid ringing bells,
Treble voices echo from open casement windows.

Today it is colder
Quiet along this path
Through autumn darkened oaks
In the shadow of gray stone.

The tourists near me pause.
Silently we look up
As low-flying helicopters
Roar from the sky.

In the bishop's garden
Birds in the holly bushes call aloud
Responding to a high flying F-16
Visible above us, through placid autumn sky:
     Circling

In the woods, leaves begin
Their yearly spiral to the ground
Responding to the first real wind of autumn.

Sunlight dapples on old beech trees
Their thick roots digging deep,
Great fingers
       Grasping the soil.
Their silver bark reflecting in its color
The gray stone skin of the cathedral façade,
      Young skin,
Stretched over shapes eight hundred years old,
Enclosing a silent space that echoes
With clashing symbols:

National
               House of Prayer for All
Battle hymns
             Way of Peace
Patriot's flag
          Crucifix:
          Suffering Love

Where at Evensong today
The choir will sing,

      As for centuries
      In scattered churches
      Of this civilization
      Choirs have sung at evening:

Only in Thee
Can we live in
    Safety.

*

And let all the people say "Amen"
<u>Psalm</u> 106: 48

*

Evensong

I : Before the Music

Gathered, not speaking, we share
      An un-breathed prayer.
Breathing in
      Soft wood, pearl stone,
      Grey-blue rose light
      High, echo-less vault
Suspended, still, awaiting
      Still unsounded song.

II.   Procession

Someone sees them coming, stands.
We rise together, watch
Growing children, white robed,
      young faces shining,
In disciplined pairs,
Following a cross.
As if
A symbol so compromised
Could still bear promise,
      Still draw together
      A people, for a song
As if. . .

III.   Inside the Music

The choirmaster raises his arms and smiles.
The choir beams back,
As if there really were
      An unheard love song,
        Singing all the time
As if
These voices, in this moment, could give
      Body to that song, as if
A window opened, and we all heard it clearly.
As if, inside the singing
      washed in children's voices
We could entrust ourselves to the soaring melody
As if it could carry us
      like a gentle current
                or a gathering wave
All the way in
          to *Yes*. . . . . to *Amen*.